So, You Want to Be an Actor?

Insider Secrets Revealed

Interactive eBook

Insider Secrets Revealed

So, You Want to Be an Actor?

Hollywood Life

ACTING IS BEHAVING TRUTHFULLY
#MOMSOFACTORS
UNDER IMAGINARY CIRCUMSTANCES.

scene heading
EXT. EDGE - NIGHT

action
Zach shivers and turns to the BOUNCER.

ZACH — character name
How much longer
until you let me in?

dialogue
BOUNCER
Look man, we just
opened. We don't have
space for everyone

BY CAMILLA MOTTE

Introduction

We are very excited that you decided to purchase a copy of **"So, You Want Be an Actor"** – *Insider Secrets Revealed*. Aspiring actors who have purchased, read, and implemented our suggestions are super intuitive. Why not find out the truth about the industry from someone who's already been there?

Actors are booking commercials, feature films, television shows, and more. So, you are making the right decision by getting educated on the business. Actors are signing contracts with agents across the board, which is increasing their resumé and income.

Our ebook aids aspiring actors and even parents in becoming more knowledgeable in the industry. You will embark on this journey with the confidence you need to succeed.

The information that I'm sharing with you is a powerful tool to have on-hand. There is a lot of information on the internet, but you won't find information like what we are providing.

We have first-hand knowledge of the industry and what goes on behind the scenes. We are providing real details and true opinions.

We are also opening up a <u>private Q & A</u> for you to submit any questions or concerns you may have.

We are super proud that you took the time to make an informed decision for yourself or your child. Sometimes things look super cool on the television and super easy, but I'll be the first to tell you, "All that Glitters Isn't Gold."

With over 160,000 union actors in the United States, this is a lucrative, but challenging career. Many people decide to drop everything and move to "**The City of Angels**," to see if they can make their dreams come true.

I'm a mom with a vision to help other people who have dreams of getting into this business. I'm not here to deter you or talk negative about the business. I'm not here to sugar coat anything either. I am here to give you my very best research and hands-on experience, so you can make the best decision for you.

This is a life long decision and you don't want to go into it blindsided. Sit back, Get a cup of Coffee, and "Let's Ride."

Contents

Chapter 1

"Our Story"

It all started in Houston, Texas, while walking through the mall in our small suburbian city. I noticed a sign that stated the mall would be having a beauty pageant. Therefore, I stopped and gathered some information about the upcoming pageant to take home.

We decided to enter our daughter into the contest on a whim – why not? Let's see what happens.

We were very green to the entire pageant situation. Even though we had no real idea what "a pageant" was all about, we set out to pay our registration fees and follow the information packet handed to us.

The only items we needed to purchase was a formal dress and shoes. Entering the pageant blindfolded wasn't a big deal because our daughter came with the cuteness, so that wouldn't cost anything. LOL.

Nevertheless, longer story-short, she entered the contest and unbeknown to us she won the entire contest. She won her first "Beauty Queen," title. We were shocked to say the least. We had no earthly idea this would have been the outcome. We knew she was our adorable little girl, but we didn't realize what had just happened. Yes, it sounds as if I had a big head, but I didn't.

As I stated before, I was very green at the entire concept. Consequently, our daughter came home with 5 trophies, Beauty Queen, Best Hair, Best Eyes, and well, I don't remember all of them.

 Fast forward -- my husbands co-worker told us about an upcoming competition that he heard about where this company would train children to compete in Los Angeles and New York. My first thought was that it was a scam, but I went simply to see what was going on with this event in Houston, Texas.

OMG ! There were so many people waiting and the line was wrapped around the building. If you know anything about Houston, you know it was crazy hot outside too.

Nevertheless, we proceeded to get out of our car. I was very reluctant to get out of the car because I didn't feel like standing in that long line.

Eventually, I became very tired of sitting in the long line, but just about when I was about to call it quits, this young man walked out of the building and passed everyone up, but stopped to offer me and my daughter a bottle of water.

I looked up at him with big eyes and said, "sure, thank you," so I sat down and thought to myself, "O.K., God must want us to stay in this line for a reason."

Nonetheless, the line moved quickly along. There were over 500 people waiting to audition for the Los Angeles training. When we finally made our way inside the building, the training staff explained that they were aiming to take 50 people to Los Angeles.

They explained that they would train them to model, act, compete to win prizes, and have an opportunity to get a booking agent and/or manager for the L.A. market. This particular event happens in New York as well, but we were only training to compete in Los Angeles.

You probably guessed it ! We were one of the 50 candidates chosen to compete in Los Angeles and once again, we were very surprised. Our daughter, Wendi, competed at the competition in L.A. in 2007, once again, she won just about every category she entered.

We were very surprised, but extremely proud of her. This seemed to be her thing. She loved the pageants and she loved performing at the competition in Los Angeles.

We stayed at the Western Boneventure Hotel, Los Angeles, CA for an entire week. The hotel and event was extremely nice and we had so much fun during the super busy week. We met many friends whom we are still friends with to this very day.

We paid a lot of money to be entered into this event, but I wouldn't have changed a thing. The only thing I might do differently is to let other people know they don't have to spend as much money as we did. We didn't know any better, but we do believe the experience of the event helped our daughter get to where she is today.

Nevertheless, this book, in our opinion, will do more for you than entering a contest and spending thousands upon thousands of dollars.

You can save your money for acting or dance classes, books, headshots, rent, gas, audition clothes, acting publications, etc. I can think of so many things the money we spent on the training fee would have come in handy for, but it was worth the experience.

Also, she's now considered an ALUM with a lot of other celebs that came from the same event like: Ashton Kutcher, Ashley Greene,

Eva Longoria, Jessica Biel, Katie Holmes, Logan Browning, Wendi Motte, and many more.

Eva Longoria

We have been living between Los Angeles and Texas since 2007. We have made friends with so many people in L.A. Most of our friends are like extended family. We've gone through a lot of ups and a lot of downs while living in L.A and being in the industry. You wouldn't believe the things we have gone through while living in L.A. It has been a three ringed circus, **LITERALLY**.

The hardest part of living in L.A was leaving my home that I've known all my life. Also, leaving my husband behind was difficult as well. I've seen so many marriages break up between parents who have chosen to live the same life that we are living now. It's really difficult and you have to be a special kind of person to take on this life.

We are believers and we always put God first in all decisions. We have been blessed and we have been a blessing. God has taken

7

us from the back to the front and from the front to the back. Never settle and Never get a big head because you can be dropped on your bottom very quickly. You may soon find out-- there is not much loyalty out here in these L.A. streets.

Everyone has a different journey, and this is our journey to share with you.

Keep your head up and if this is what you want, don't let anyone or anything (not even family) talk you out of living your dream and LIVING your best life. We are testaments that dreams do come true.

Here is my devotion to you:

If you have any questions at any time and you want to send me an inquiry. I'm giving you my personal contact information. Seriously, I know what it's like to be in a new state and be all alone or at least seem alone with no help and no family. Now, we are family.

If I can help you in this process, I will do so. Here is my contact information.

Email :

Love and BLESSINGS,

Camilla

Ritz Crackerful Commercial

Filming Zeroes 2

Are you certain you want to be an actor?

In this section we simply want you to think about the reasons you want to become an actor. Acting is a huge step, because it's what most people would call an **unconventional** career.

> **"Unconventional jobs** can include **careers** that are out of the ordinary as well as **careers** that may involve unusual tasks, schedules or work environments."

Acting is more than a typical career, it's a lifestyle that you need to commit to. On the usual side of the business, booking gigs doesn't happen fast.

However, there are always unusual occurrences that you hear about in which a new person will come on the acting scene and book a major movie role and their career takes off instantaneously.

Acting career statistics for most people is about 7-10 years or more.

Here are a few ideas that I've come up with to help you decide if you want to become an actor:

➢ You are fascinated with the acting industry as whole. You identify with the characters on your favorite T.V. shows. You think to yourself, "Hey, I could have played this role." or "this particular (naming a celebrity) character/actor could have acted out this role."

➢ You feel compassion when you think about acting. You feel as if you can become a world changer through your art. You know deep down inside, that you long to fulfill this dream of becoming an actor.

➢ You were part of the drama team at your high school or college and you received so many compliments that you did so well in your performances. People told you that your performance was believable and they were taken back by how well you portrayed that particular character.

➢ If you think about acting so much that you find yourself constantly doing research on the topic. You find ways to put yourself in the path of others who have similar career goals as you do. You have passion for the art and It's almost busting at the seams.

➢ Lastly, do you enjoy making Youtube videos? People find you funny and intriguing. You have loyal followers that provide comments that are positive and uplifting. We aren't talking about the trolls who look for everything bad. We are talking about people who appreciate the art that you create.

If you can relate to any of the ideas above then continue reading, but never ever compare yourself to others.

You be the best YOU, that you can be.

I'm confident that you know what you want and when you put your mind to it, nothing will stop you from becoming exactly what you want.

No matter what comes at you – Stay Positive ! !

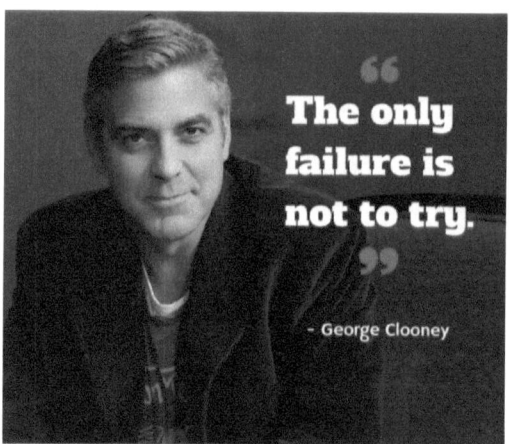

Chapter 3

How much money is needed to live in Los Angeles?

Los Angeles is the second-largest city in the United States of America. It's called The Sunshine State for a reason. Many people long to live in Sunny California. They move to Los Angeles because they have big dreams they want to fulfill.

The entertainment industry is multi-billion-dollar industry. People move to the Los Angeles area for many reasons.

Here are a few TOP reasons most people move to L.A.:

- ✓ **To attend a college or University**
- ✓ **To become an actor or actress**
- ✓ **To become a director or producer**
- ✓ **To become a screenwriter**
- ✓ **For a change of scenery**
- ✓ **To get away from the normal mundane life**

There are many other reasons people choose this particular city. We chose L.A because our daughter loved being in her element of the entertainment industry. She loves the connections made with other young children who have the same mindset as she does.

The Economy:

Los Angeles has a vast economy. Therefore, prices are extremely high for land and housing, including rental property. You can expect to pay a pretty penny for utilities, rent, food, and gas. So, please be prepared and informed because you will be shelling out some serious cash if you move to the "City of Angels."

Average Rent: Average cost of rent in the Los Angeles area is as follows:

- ❖ **One Bedroom Apartment – $2100 per month**
- ❖ **Two Bedroom Apartment – $2600 per month**
- ❖ **Three Bedroom Apartment – $3500 per month**

Don't let the prices above scare you away entirely. There are ways around some of these costs. If you decide to get a roommate, you won't have to pay as much. Also, various areas of the city have different prices attached to the rental. You might even find a house to rent for around the same price and you may be able to rent out a room or two if your landlord approves. Another idea is to move outside the City of Los Angeles and you may be able to reduce your rent about $500 or more. However, please take into consideration that you get what you pay for.

 **Utilities**: This is one of those things that can be good and bad. What I've found is that, in Los Angeles, during certain months, you won't need to run the A/C. Whether or not you have to run the A/C is contingent upon where you live and where your apartment or residence is situated.

You may be able to get away with a fairly decent utility bill. The average cost of utilities is approximately $125 per month for a 900 square foot apartment.

However, you will want to do what you can about conserving as much energy as possible. I do laundry at least once a week and pretty much always after 6 p.m. It's a lot cooler outside in the evening time; therefore, I'm not using as much energy as I would if I washed clothes during the daytime and it's 95 degrees outside.

You gotta think smarter. Most of my cooking is done in the evening as well. You simply have to plan your routine and usage. It's not that hard to try and keep your bills down to a minimum.

 **Transportation**: The city of Los Angeles is very busy and the traffic is horrendous, but you can find ways around all of that to a certain degree.

Methods of transportation

> - Your own personal vehicle
> - RideShare Programs
> - Carpool
> - Bus transportation
> - Bicycling
> - Walking

Rideshare programs are in high demand all around California because people do not want to deal with driving in traffic every day. The average cost to use one of the rideshare programs is

(Lyft - $1.06 per mile, plus $2.30 service fee). Prices are subject to change at company's discretion. It's definitely worth your time to research the other companies and transportation methods.

It's very costly to maintain your own personal vehicle, but if you are like me, I can't be without my own personal vehicle. I don't mind taking a ride share to the airport or an event, but if I'm just running errands around town and going to auditions, then I must have my own mode of transportation.

Total Living Cost Needed for about 5-6 months :

 It's a good idea to save about $8k-- $10,000 dollars so that you will be able to live comfortably starting out. I'm sure there are places to live just to get by temporarily, but I'm not that mom. I'm only going to give examples of how we live.

We believe in comfort and safety. Not everyone lives the same way, but after living in Los Angeles for 8 years, then back home to my cushy home in Texas, then back to L.A., I have some special requests. For example, I will not go without a washer/dryer. No questions asked. There are things that **I WILL NOT** skimp on.

Chapter 4

Lodging

Los Angeles is a beautiful place to live or visit, but it is like a needle in a haystack trying to find a decent place to stay. You have to deal with 21st century situations, like lack of good customer service, that can be a bit of a headache.

When we first moved to L.A. in 2007, it was easy to find a place to stay, but fast forward to 2019, OMG ! What a headache! One would think with technology advancing at the speed of light, it would be so much easier to find a place to live. NOT ! It was easier 13 years ago.

Today, almost no one answers the phone when calling to locate housing. I kept getting voice mails that no one returned. What in the world is going on over there in L.A.? One might think someone would want to lease an apartment, but to my demise, not many people answer the phones or return phone calls these days. I'm really big on providing excellent customer service, but apparently, not everyone shares my view.

I feel like we have a bit of advantage than a lot of people who are simply starting from scratch. We lived in the Los Angeles area from 2007- 2015. We moved back home to Texas in 2015. Therefore, we knew most of the areas in which to look for places that were somewhat nice and safe.

Good areas to Live tha are near auditions:

There are many areas that you can live in, but here is a short list of the areas that are pretty close to most of the auditions, etc.

- ✓ Burbank
- ✓ Studio City
- ✓ Sherman Oaks
- ✓ North Hollywood
- ✓ Valley Village
- ✓ Santa Monica
- ✓ West Hollywood

It's a good idea to have some sort of connections in Los Angeles before moving to the city. Anyone can make a photo look extremely well with a fisheye lens, but when you arrive it is a dump and you may have already sank a lot of money into it.

Remember, once you put down a deposit, it's normally non-refundable. Trust me, I have seen some dumps in L.A. One area could be nice and when you drive up the block, there could be homeless people walking around and living in tents all over the place. One thing I do know about L.A is that they do not have a handle on their homeless population.

 These unfortunate individuals can be seen pretty much all over the city, except some of the nicher suburbian areas. It seems like the homeless population grows more and more every year. Don't get me wrong when I mention homeless people on the streets. Thieves and robbers can drive anywhere they choose to strike as well.

If you are able to hire someone to look at apartments for you, it would be a great idea to consider.

Please don't trust a photo alone. Also, don't rely on all of the reviews you may find online, including YELP. No offense YELP. I think some people give bad reviews just to give bad reviews.

I'm sure you've heard of the, "Review Trolls." Some reviews are legit, I'm sure; but a whole lot of them are bogus.

To wrap this section up-- you should be looking at paying anywhere from $1200 for a small studio apartment, $1800-$2000 for a 1 bedroom, $2500+ for a 2 bedroom.

The former prices are for modest living only. There are apartments that are a lot more expensive and some that are somewhat less expensive. All prices quoted is non-furnished and doesn't include utilities.

Roommate Option:

You always have an option of finding a roommate. You can look for a roommate online if you wish, by word of mouth, or referrals. I've seen lots of online ads for roommates. Honestly, I wouldn't look on Craigslist for a roommate. I don't know, after seeing the Lifetime movie, 'The Craigslist Killer," anything Craigslist gives me the shakes. LOL

Also, you have to be a roommate kind of person in order to deal with that situation. I'm not a good person to ask because I have little patience for trying to clean up after grown people, and I'm not trying to be mommy to a grown person. I love you, but no thanks. Good luck on that one. I'm rooting for you.

Courtney Biggs, Ariel Winter, Wendi Motte

Chapter 5

Business or Hobby?

When you decide to get into the entertainment business, you must realize you are in business; and therefore, you must treat it as such. Just about everyone you will encounter will be connected to the industry in some shape, form, or fashion. Other aspiring actors are serious about what they do too.

This is how...

- ✓ their families are supported
- ✓ they pay their bills
- ✓ food is put on the table
- ✓ parents put their children through college

You must treat your acting career just as a doctor, lawyer, pro football/basketball player treat their careers. If you make a misstep, you or your family may get put out on your butt. The movie industry is a $40 billion dollar a year business in the U.S. alone. This sound extremely serious to me, doesn't it to you?

You must remain professional at all times. Your social media must remain professional at all times. Since we are in the times of social influencers and the fact that just about anything can be found on the internet. You must <u>make it your businesss</u> to keep your nose clean and on your business.

> *Successful people never worry about what others are doing.*

Justice Models, including Wendi Motte

Just like a regular 9-5 job, you must show up to work on-time, right? Hence, you must show up to your auditions on-time or better yet, **EARLY**.

If you're early, you are on-time, if you are on-time, you are late, if you are late, it's inexcusable

---

You must be cordial and be able to work well with other employees. This equates to working well with your fellow actors/actresses. No time for drama or divas. Directors and producers like their sets to be drama free, if that's possible.

If you don't treat people good and act professional, you can and will be replaced immediately. The studios have one common goal, to make movies and produce blockbusters. If they provided you an opportunity, then you are blessed and should honor that blessing.

27

Chapter 6

Get a Temporary Job
"The bills must get paid"

Upon moving into your new residence, one of the very first things you need to do is start looking for a job. It would be a smart idea to do this before you get to Los Angeles, but if you've saved up a little nest egg, then start looking for *temporary* work the moment you get settled into your new pad.

Sad, but true. If you are not employed upon arriving to Los Angeles, it is imperative that you make this a high priority on your list. It's few and far between that you will automatically land a job the moment you arrive in L.A.

Therefore, you will need to do what you can to keep a roof over your head, gas in your car, and food in your stomach. The

 homeless population is too real out in these L.A. streets and I do not want you are me to become part of this crisis.

Most auditions will typically take place for adults in the morning or afternoon, and mainly in the afternoon for younger children. Therefore, it's probably best to look for a temporary job that has evening hours available, if possible.

When looking for a job, be sure to search for a job that will be flexible with your potential acting schedule. You need to pay the bills, but don't lose sight of the reason you moved to L.A. Be open and honest with your potential employer. Let them know you are an actor/actress and there may be times where you need to take time off for an audition and/or bookings.

You want to be honest with your employer so that you don't put them out and they don't put you out as well. Remember, it's a two-way street. Nobody wants their time wasted. Please don't burn bridges either.

Continue working on your craft, as well as maintaining your part-time or temporary job. **Acting takes time**. The statistics that we were hit with when we moved to Los Angeles was that for every 50 auditions, you may (not will) book one (1) job.

For you Mathematicians that's a ratio of 50:1

Realistically, it can take anywhere from 8-10 years – at a consistent pace before you actually become what's called "a working actor."

Working actor means --you are in like flinn and not having to hit the pavement as hard to book a job. This is the point where casting directors, executives, and producers know who you are and are comfortable with your work.

Once this happens, you will work almost non-stop. This is where you want to be. This is the **GOAL**. This can and does happen all the time, but it doesn't happen overnight. You need to have staying power. You need to have tough skin to stay in this game.

Please don't expect to become an overnight success. My purpose in writing this book is for you to know exactly what you are getting into.

good things
take time...

Temporary Job Idea Listing

- ❖ Personal Trainer
- ❖ Fitness Instructor
- ❖ Bar Tender
- ❖ Nanny
- ❖ Waiter/Waitress
- ❖ Dog Walker
- ❖ Tutor
- ❖ Freelance Writer/Blogger
- ❖ Uber/Lyft Ride Share Driver
- ❖ Mall Salesperson
- ❖ Temporary/Part-time Office Assistant
- ❖ Amazon Seller
- ❖ E-Bay Seller
- ❖ Virtual Assistant
- ❖ Substitute Teacher
- ❖ Part-Time Coach (Local School)
- ❖ Acting or Singing Coach (Must be trained)
- ❖ Party Planner
- ❖ Photographer
- ❖ Dance Instructor

Chapter 7

Auditions

Most of your auditions will be held either in the morning or in the afternoon. A lot of the auditions vary due to the persons age category. Auditions for younger children are usually held in the afternoon, due to school. A large majority of the children in Los

 Angeles are homeschooled, but the casting directors do take it into consideration that your child may be in public school so they hold most of the younger children's auditions later in the afternoon.

As far as the young adults and adults are concerned, most of those auditions are either in the morning or early afternoon. Nevertheless, many of the auditions are done and over with by 6 p.m. No one wants to be caught in L.A. traffic, if at all possible, so the casting directors will audition you and have you out of there really quickly.

It will take you longer to drive to an audition than it will to actually audition with the casting directors. Auditions may take 5-10 minutes at the most.

Headshots

Even though most of the Casting Directors no longer ask for headshots, it's a good idea to set up a photoshoot for professional photos and print about 20-30 headshots at a time to keep on-hand. Sometimes you will need them, but most of the time you won't. Headshots used to be a huge expense in the industry, but now that technology has taken over, they are not widely used in auditions and printed as much as they were in the past. I'm sure the lack of headshot use affected a whole lot of local headshot print businesses, but at least headshots are not obsolete. Headshots will come in handy for a lot of situations and we will always need photographers.

Here are a few ways you may need to utilize headshots:

- ✓ Marketing Materials like
- ✓ Your Acting Website
- ✓ Your Online Casting Profiles
- ✓ Agent or Manager Submissions
- ✓ To give to your fans at press events

Chapter 8

Handeling Rejection

We live in a society where the internet has totally ruined us. There are so many internet trolls out there taking stabs and dabs at everyone they possibly can; therefore, things are so much harder now than it was 15-20 years ago. We are all humans, and most humans crave acceptance. The fear of rejection is very real. Actors are no different than the regular Jane or Joe. Actors take their work seriously and therefore, a lot take rejection personally. I'm so glad my daughter and I learned at a young age, not to take rejection as the end of the world. The acting world is a cold cold world, so as Sean "Puff Daddy" Combs says, "It's a cold

world, bundle Up."

It's very true. Not only has the internet ruined us, but it changed a lot of other things in this society too. Everyone seems to get their feelings hurt at the smallest escapade. Rejection is a part of life. Rejection is part of the learning process. As I was often told, rejection is God's protection. So, if you find another way to look at rejection then it won't sting so badly.

In the acting world, each audition is extremely important so actors try their best to go in the audition and **KILL IT** the first time. Most of the time, you will KILL IT, but guess what? Majority of the time, it's not even about you.

It's not about you doing good, bad, or indifferent. Sometimes, the casting directors or their clients don't really know what they want at the time of the audition. They are looking for fresh ideas and faces to match characters.

Casting directors are looking for something to jump out at them. Sometimes, they don't know that much. Majority of the time, they have an idea, a script, and some time on their hands to start the ball rolling.

They call hundreds of actors in for an audition and then somebody comes along and pulls the rug right from underneath the entire project and it's just toast at that point. So, all that worrying you did doesn't matter one bit. It's best to prepare for every audition, go in and do your very best.

Finally, when you walk out of that door, take a deep breath, smile, gather yourself, go use the restroom, drink some water, get in your car, say a prayer, turn on some jamz, and rock out all the way home. This isn't your first audition and it won't be your last.

Remember, the best way to overcome things that you fear is to face them head on. Have you ever heard of the word fear used as an acronym?

False
Evidence
Appearing
Real

Doesn't that make sense? Now don't fear, what's not going to kill you will make you stronger. You've got this !

Chapter 9

How to Get an Agent or Manager

Finding an acting agent is easier than you think. First of all, you need to prepare yourself for the marathon. What? You said you didn't sign up for a marathon ! Uh Oh ! Yes, you did. It's the Acting Marathon.

Always be prepared and ready to listen and learn. Remember when we talked about staying prepared by taking classes, reading, writings, etc? Well, that's what you are going to do to get an agent—stay prepared.

Acting Classes:

One way to get an agent is to enroll in an acting class. Most of the acting schools or classes will have something called Agent Night, Agent Review, or an Acting Showcase. During these events, you will have prepared a commercial, skit, and/or a monologue.

You will perform what you learned, in your class, for a bunch of invited guests of the acting studio.

The acting studio should be well connected with the industry. They should have a bunch of agents and managers that they personally know and have made connections with them.

These agents and managers will talke time out of their night to go and watch these performances in hopes to find their next big thing.

At the end of the evening, some of the agents and managers will stay after to mingle, meet, and greet some of the studio clients/actors. You will want to put on a happy face and talk to these industry professionals. This is one of the best ways to get seen by top agents in the industry.

So, make sure you check around before going into just any acting school that you find on the internet. Make sure there are references and referrals available.

Also, a good idea would be to go to a **FREE** class and look around, talk, and even take pictures of any actors that may be on the wall. This will give you an idea of what kind of acting school it is. Go home and do your research. Look up the names of these actors and see what projects they have and are doing currently. Don't just go to an acting school because so and so's family member is the owner. This may not help you in any way, shape, or form.

Referrals:

Another way to get an agent is to ask a friend who's already signed with a certain agent. Your friend may have inside information on whether or not his or her agency is looking for actors. This may be a quick way to get your foot in the door.

However, make sure you are prepared to "*show yourself approved*" when you walk in the door. Not only are you putting yourself on the line, but most importantly you are putting your friend on the line for getting you an interview opportunity.

Please don't take that for granted. It can be difficult to be seen by really good agents.

Self-Submission:

Believe it or not, some agencies find their clients from self-submissions. This is the reason you should get some headshots made and keep them on-hand.

You can research some agencies online or get names from a friend, then use the old cart and horse and put your information in the mail. You might be very surprised, I've gotten my daughter a new TOP agent simply by submitting her headshot anc coverletter to them by mail.

Also, you may want to drop a headshot off to casting offices if they allow drop-offs. Sometimes the casting associate may be

42

passing by at the same time you are dropping off your

headshot and you may catch their eye, so be prepared. They

may stop what they're doing and call you right in. Dress

appropriately and professionally.

Get the facts Jack ! I want you to be successful. NO one has

time for playing games. Let's get on this horse and ride it till you

can't ride no more.

Remember, YOU can do this. I'm for YOU

Your Team

Agent and Managers

Here is a quick lesson on agents and managers. You can decide whether you need one or both. Let's talk about the difference between the two.

Agents:

An agent is licensed by whatever state they are conducting their representation business. Agents must work at a physical location, not their home. The agent's job is to solicit employment opportunities for their clients, which includes you.

Agents normally take 10% commission when you get paid from a booking gig. Remember, the agent only gets paid when you get paid. Specifically, before you get paid.

Some agents have a small client base and some have a larger client base. Most actors will sign a yearly contract with the agency.

Managers:

Managers simply manage the actor's career. Managers do not have to be licensed by the state. Managers are not allowed to set up auditions or negotiate contracts.

Managers give advice, counsel, and direct the actor's career. Managers <u>can</u> work out of their home or office. Managers provide a more personal relationship with their clients.

A normal fees for a manager is 10-20% commission ONLY after you have been paid. Actually, this comes off the top before you see your paycheck. Managers, typically sign clients to a 2-3 year contract. Most managers are connected with several agents in your area. When agents have clients that need to represented, the agent may refer the client to one of their list of managers.

Managers can assist you with one-on-one personal situations. I'm sure you have seen managers on T.V. who represent basketball and football players.

Sports managers are pretty much hands-on in keeping their client's noses clean and to the grind. Being a manager for a pro player can sometimes seem like a super dee duper headache, but I guess they are making enough money to deal with those headaches.

I hope this explains the process and duties of agents vs managers. It can be a bit confusing at times. We have met many people that only have a manager and we've met many people that have agents, managers, publicists, representatives, etc

OH MY ! ! I hope they are left with something at the end of that long entourage.

We previously asked if it was necessary to have a manager and people often told us, "a manager is needed only **IF** there's something to manage." I don't know if that was a stab in the dark, but I took it to mean, NOPE, not right now we didn't. So, I opted to keep our money just a little bit longer.

Debby Ryan & Wendi Motte

Chapter 11

Industry Publications

This is not going to be a very detailed chapter, but I thought it is necessary to mention the fact that actors should read a few industry publications on the market. I don't mean the tabloids, I truly mean industry publications.

I want you to stay up to date on important situations going on in your world. Yes, we are already claiming the victory. I don't work for any of these companies, I'm just putting as much pertinent information in this eBook that I possibly can, because I'm for you and I want you to WIN! WINNING!

Four Industry Publications:

1. SAG/AFTRA Magazine – Quarterly Magazine. Once you become a member of the union, you will get this magazine mailed to your home as part of your membership. It's chocked full of good information about the entertainment industry, but mainly geared towards SAG/AFTRA members.

2. <u>Hollywood Reporter</u> – Entertainment News. Hard copy and Online Subscriptions. You may see these in your agents offices too. Also, you can log in online and sign up for their email newsletter.

3. <u>Variety Magazine</u> – Entertainment News. There is an online and newsletter subscription available. Their basic subscription will cost you $119 per year. Most agents and managers will have a copy of this in their office.

4. <u>IMDB</u> – Internet Movie Database. A FREE online database of information related to films, television programs, home videos, video games, and streaming content online. The paid version includes cast, production crew and personal biographies, plot summaries, trivia, fan and critical reviews, and ratings.

By reading these publications, you will stay abreast ot what's going on in the acting world around you. You will find lots of information about actors, tv shows, movies, and any news that you will need to know about. It's always better to stay informed in whatever industry in which you are involved.

Getting Yourself Noticed

The entertainment industry has changed a bunch over the past 5-10 years. Therefore, you need to come alive and help make this acting thing work for **YOU**. You must have your own determination and an "I won't take NO for an answer,".

So, let's get after what you should do as a new actor coming into the game.

- ➢ Being persistent is first and foremost. Most actors wait around for their agents or managers to call them for an audition. With all the technology at your disposal, you need to follow-through during your down-time.

    - o Actors must learn to send follow-up emails to industry professionals who can assist them in advancing their career. You must consistently follow through with every connection you've made in the industry. You will begin seeing results as time goes by.

- ➢ Make your own blog, Vlog, or website. Use these varied platforms to make videos of yourself. You need to show the casting directors and agents your personality.
- ➢ Make a **YouTube** channel and get creative with the channel. There are a lot of people who became famous on their youtube channels. These people can be seen on movies and t.v. The studios want influencers in their projects too.

    - ➢ Create your own video projects. Get with your friends and create your own movie reel. This can be as simple as gathering a few actor friends and simply recording a segment of you all just talking and having a good time.

This will show the real you, as opposed to the acting persona.
- ➤ Align yourself with talented industry professionals who have the different skills than you do. Make friends.
- ➤ Do short films with college or university film students.

The biggest take-away here is to create content. The more content you create, the quicker you will get noticed by casting directors, producers, and directors.

You might not believe this, but now, you have the power to make yourself famous, popular, and rich. Why wait around for other people to do 1/10 the job for you?   The fact that you created the content will get you noticed faster than any co-starring role can.

Wendi Motte & Taylor Lautner

Chapter 13

Create a Contact List

It is very important that you try to stay as organized as possible. These days it's easier than ever to get used to being a more organized person. I can remember not being very organized, but the older I get, the more I strive for organization.

The acting business is a business where you will come in contact with many people who you don't want to forget. Any contact you make could be a contact that you want to keep for years to come. You never know when you might need to pull a name and number out of your hat and use it.

I have been in the grocery store just walking around and I'll strike up a conversation with someone and low and behold that simple conversation became a full on contact. The person you are talking to might not be a direct contact, but they may have a friend who has a friend who knows a friend who is in the business and looking for someone for an up and coming movie.

Quick story:

My husband and I was walking around Trader Joe's (local health food grocery store) and I complimented a lady on her outfit. Her husband made a joke about how I shouldn't have complimented her. We laughed, started talking to one another and long-story short, the husband is in the industry and he knew someone who was about to make a movie and was looking for actors for the movie. I boldly asked him for his contact persons info. He gave it to me. I followed up and he sent my daughter a script for her to submit an online audition.

See, something as simple as that turned into a chance for my daughter to be put in front of a casting director. If I hadn't given this lady a compliment and I stayed in my own lane, I wouldn't have been able to make that contact.

So, next time you are in an elevator, don't put your head down and not speak to anyone. Look up, make eye contact, and say hello. You never know who's in that elevator with you.

Now where was I? Oh yeah, create a contact list for the acting industry in your phone, but please make a back up hard copy. If your phone crashes or you lose it then you will be lost for crucial information.

I believe mobile phones are great, but I don't wholeheartedly trust them. Keep names, address, emails, social media accounts, and phone numbers in your phone and also in a notebook.

Also, you may want ot add a notes section so that you can jog your memory about where and how you met that person. You never know, if you contact them, they may not remember how they met you and therefore you can help jog their memory. They will be very appreciative that you took so much time and detail in remembering who they are and how you both met.

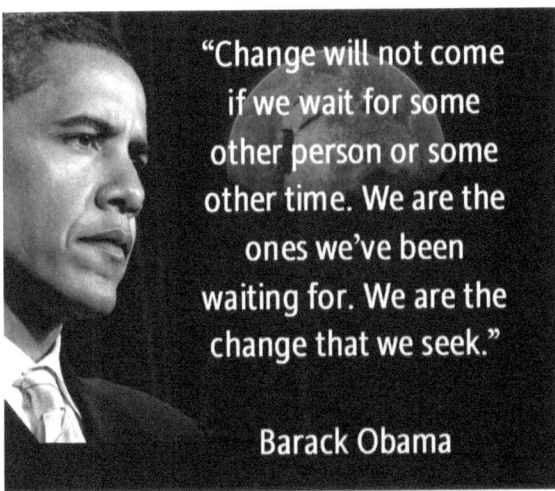

"Change will not come if we wait for some other person or some other time. We are the ones we've been waiting for. We are the change that we seek."

Barack Obama

Chapter 14

Always Work on Your Craft

Let's jump right in the water with both feet. Acting is similar to being an athlete. Serious athletes are always training and working to stay in shape whether they are in season or off season.

Athletes must have consistent training to stay good at what they do. They can't simply work out a day or two before the big game and expect to bring their "A" game, right? Right, so they have to have on-going training.

What about singers? Do you think Beyonce' Jennifer Lopez, Ariana Grande, and John Legend take singing lessons? Do you think they have rehearsals before the performance? Do they just go out in front of a crowd of 100K+ people without having trained?

Absolutey not ! Such is the same for actors. Actors must always strive to keep learning and enhancing their craft.

You will find even the most seasoned actors taking an acting class before a big performance so they can ace the role without a doubt in anyone's mind that the character they are portraying is real.

Hence, this is what you will need to do as well.

You will need to always work on your craft. You will need to set aside some money and time to make this happen on a consistent basis.

Acting classes aren't cheap either. However, it's best to ask around and get some referrals. Private Coaching isn't the area where I would just open an internet browser and play a guessing game with who's name sounds like they might be a good acting coach.

Trust me, if you are in the entertainment industry, the people you come in contact with will know some good coaches and some not so good coaches. Ask for the good ones. LOL

Here are three (3) FREE ways help improve your craft:

1. Write – Yes, you didn't take all those English classes in elementary through college for nothing. And you thought you'd never use that stuff. Writing is creative. You should get a journal and strive write in it every day. Don't worry about spelling or grammar at this point –**JUST WRITE**. Get those creative juices flowing. Make writing fun. Take your journal with you to your favorite coffee spot, even on your balcony and just write for 10 minutes without giving it much thought. Don't worry about punctuation either. If you do this at least 5 days a week (yeah, I'm giving you a two day break), then you will find that writing will help you grow to a new level. Heck, one day you might even write a screenplay. Watch out there now!

2. Read – Yup, you thought you wouldn't do that after school either, right? Well, you've had enough time off. You want to be an actor so pick up a book and read. Actors read so you should read. Oh, did I say actors read? Yes, sometimes they

have a 100-page script to memorize or more. This is your new normal. You should expect to read at least 15-30 minutes every single day. No, not giving you a break here. Read silently and most importantly - - **READ ALOUD**. Pretend you are reading a story to a child, a friend, or a neighbor. You need to hear yourself read. Look for different types of reading material. You can read books, magazines, the internet, or the bible. Whatever you do, read something you are interested in and that you enjoy. **P.S.** Reading Instagram text or Tweets from Twitter does not count towards your reading.

3. Lastly, Practice Memorization. This is where you can search the internet for **FREE** monologues, commercials, or even poems. Read them over and over again until you have it memorized. This will exercise your memorization skills. Actors do a lot of memorization and if you are serious about the business of acting, then you will need to memorize your lines when you book your next feature film. If you need to go out

and purchase some GINKO vitamins to aid your memory,

then that's o.k. too

Alyson Stoner & Wendi Motte

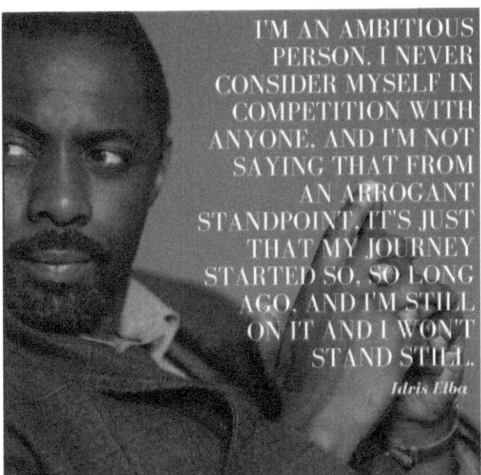

Chapter 15

Taxes

This business is no different than any other business or job. Uncle Sam wants a piece of the pie too. One unfortunate thing about living in California is that you will not only have to pay Federal taxes, you will have to pay state taxes as well.

 You will be able to write-off a good deal of your expenses such as, headshots, gas, travel, acting classes, union dues, gifts to agents, special audition clothes, etc.

Be sure to keep accurate records of both your income and expenses. This will make it so much better for your tax advisors.

Always be sure to consult your tax advisor with any specific questions you have regarding taxable items.

There are a number of expenses that will be tax deductible so be sure and keep all of your receipts. You won't be able to use all of them, but better safe than sorry, right? It's also a good idea to keep track of your income and expenses by creating a simple spreadsheet.

Actors are considered Sole Proprietors, but it's not necessary that you file an LLC, but you may have to use a Schedule C to itemize your deductions. This is a little more detailed than I want to get right now, but just keep that in your back pocket for future reference.

WEN by Chaz Dean Photoshoot

Chapter 16

Frequently Asked Questions:

1. Do I have to move to Los Angeles or New York?

   a. No, you don't HAVE to move to either right now, but if you are serious about acting you may need to make that move eventually.

2. Can I live in my home state and travel back and forth?

   a. Yes, you can do that. Just know you will need to pay for your transportation and housing for any auditions that take you out of state.

3. Is it hard to book jobs when NOT living in Los Angeles?

   a. The short answer is YES. I've met plenty of people who do it and you can too, but it is a bit more difficult.

4. How does someone find out about auditions?

   a. Search online and ask your acting agent.

5. Can I get into the acting business with no prior experience?

    a. Yes, you can. However, it's best to get some theater and/or acting experience.

6. Can someone audition for a movie without an agent?

    a. Yes, they can. It's a little difficult, but it can be done.

7. Can a minor child become an actor without parental permission?

    a. No, you must have adult consent and supervision.

8. Is it easy to work as a background actor?

    a. Yes, it's fairly easy to work as as background actor.

9. Does background actors get paid?

    a. Yes, they do. It's minimal to an actor, but yes.

10.   Do I need an acting resumé?

    a. Not in the beginning, but you will need one eventually.

Chapter 17

Your Notes

_____

_____

_____

_____

_____

_____

_____

_____

_____

_____

DISCLAIMER

We are not lawyers. This eBook and the content provided herein are simply for educational purposes and do not take the place of legal advice from your attorney. Every effort has been made to ensure that the content provided in this eBook is accurate and helpful for our readers at publishing time. However, this is not an exhaustive treatment of the subjects. No liability is assumed for losses or damages due to the information provided. You are responsible for your own choices, actions, and results. You should consult your attorney for your specific publishing and disclaimer questions and needs.

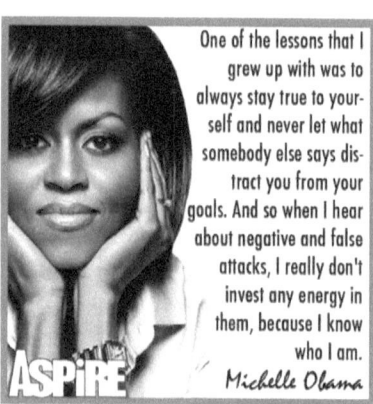

One of the lessons that I grew up with was to always stay true to yourself and never let what somebody else says distract you from your goals. And so when I hear about negative and false attacks, I really don't invest any energy in them, because I know who I am.

Michelle Obama